Wisdomics-Gracenomics: The New Monetary Paradigm and Its Policies Change Everything

Patreon

https://www.patreon.com/user?u=4749561

https://stevehummel.substack.com/publish

Introduction

This book is neither a tome nor an indecipherable blur of mathematical equations. Like wisdom itself it is a short, direct, and pungent set of discernments that can lead to deeper intellectual insights which is one of the major signatures of paradigm changes. Please read it with the enthusiasm and excitement that I have tried to imbue it with.

This book is written to enlighten the new paradigm and the policies that enable it, to visualize it as much as possible and to urge you to become an activist who will be able to take this information, communicate it and help get it rapidly implemented. Every battle is ultimately a political one and getting the new paradigm enacted will be no different. The book of rebuttals to critiques of the new economics that I call Wisdomics-Gracenomics will be released soon after this book and will also be of help in this effort.

Most essentially this book is about two things:

1) Awakening to you the greatest opportunity to enable the self-actualization of an aspect of the highest and most beneficial experience humanity has ever conceived namely, grace as in gratitude, by integrating Gifting into the universally participated in, everyday economic activity of going to the store to purchase something. Yes, that's right, as attitude is 99% of everything, gratitude is correctly preached by every self-help

guru and every one of the world's major wisdom traditions, the policy program of Wisdomics-Gracenomics potentially has the mega-paradigm change capability to be the next key step in human and temporal universe evolution, that the species has ever experienced. That's a big claim, but if you understand that the key to most effectively self-actualizing any positive experience is monitored by repeating that experience on an everyday basis, then you can see the absolute workability and potential effectiveness of creating gratitude as a response to a large percentage discount to the price of virtually everything you buy. Gifting begets gratitude. Visualize an economy of grace as in Gifting and keep on visualizing that as you read about the policy program in this book.

2) The three primary policies that change everything you think you know about economics and the money system because they are the very expression of the new paradigm itself in those studies. These policies utilize the understandings that money is

most basically accounting within which structure the entirety of the economy and the money system are embedded, and that the algebraic convention of equation is consistent with the double entry bookkeeping mechanisms of debits and credits summing to zero.

The precise expression of the new paradigm is Direct and Reciprocal Monetary Gifting, Monetary Gifting for short, and the paradigm changing policies are:

1) a 50% price discount gifted (directly) to consumers at retail sale and a (reciprocal) rebating of the totality of that discount

back to the enterprise who gave it, by the monetary authority which the legislature mandates to do precisely that,
2) a $1000/mo. universal dividend for everyone 18 years of age and older for life and
3) a second 50% discount/debt jubilee reduction at the point of loan signing for all big-ticket items and green consumer products.

When you fully see all the immediate and "knock on" effects of these three policies your understanding of economics and the monetary system will be forever changed. It is that powerful, enlightening and creatively beneficial for virtually all economic agents. Focus on it and its effects and you are way ahead of even the most erudite economic scholars. If you get these policies, you get most of everything else in the book. If you do not get it, you don't get the new paradigm. All the other details of the book and how they integrate into the economy are important as well of course, but fully understanding these three policies is the philosopher's stone that opens the mind to the temporal universe effects of the new paradigm.

Also understand that integrative thinking is the core process and means of garnering wisdom itself, so if one follows the dictum that "when in doubt integrate…and keep on integrating", they will remain on the path toward the greater truth. And it is conversely and generally true that if you stop integrating truths at the theoretical or even the philosophical level…you will fall into the dualistic and often egotistically rigid trap of obsessively claiming you know the whole truth about whatever you're discussing…when combining/integrating the truths in the two perspectives you're reviewing will generally reveal a thirdness greater oneness of truthfulness in the opposing sides of a discussion.

Whenever one comes across a part of this book that in some way is contrary to a monetary or economic belief you hold remember the following ascending scale of ways to combine knowledge and truths. Each step upward on this scale includes all and hopefully only the truths in the level below it so it's both an integrative combination and a purification process of truths that results in an increased level of knowing.

Ascending Scale of Knowledge/Epistemology (first level mentioned is lowest on the scale)

Research- the process of gathering data.

Theorizing- the logical and relevant combining of alleged to be true data and observations.

Philosophy- the logical and relevant combining of ideas and concepts including ethical considerations.

Paradigm- the single most effective applied concept that describes an entire pattern or pattern change in both the temporal universe and in the mind, and which itself is an integration of opposites. That is, of the single concept of the paradigm itself and of the operant factors and realities of the complexity/pluralness/many-ness of the pattern it relates to.

Mega-Paradigm- a paradigm change that immediately, beneficially and continuously effects the individual and the entire human species, and also has "spill over" beneficial effects in bodies of knowledge/areas of human endeavor other than the primary area of the paradigm change. Monetary Gifting is a mega-paradigm change.

Zeitgeist/Ethic of the Age- the agreed upon over-riding idea and driving force of the current or a new era.

The Three Policies That Change Everything

1) A 50% discount to the consumer at the terminal ending point of the entire productive process at retail sale on all consumer items and services, and a rebate of the entirety of that discount back to the enterprise giving it to their customers/consumers, by the monetary authority that creates all new money.

This single Gifting policy beneficially resolves the two deepest and most thorny problems of current economic theory, namely individual and systemic monetary austerity and price and asset inflation. It does this by accomplishing what is currently considered impossible, that is, increasing the supply of money while simultaneously not only ending price inflation, but beneficially integrating price deflation into profit making economic systems.

Thus, inflation and the tyranny of the money system's current monopolistic paradigm of **Debt Only** as the sole form and vehicle for the creation and distribution of credit/money will never again stop humanity from being able to adequately partake of the abundant production we are capable of and, as I will later point out with further policies, will also enable us to make the rational decisions for species and ecological survival that are even more urgently needed. Do you think accomplishing all of this and immediately doubling your purchasing power at the same time would make you feel good? Remember the power of gratitude.

A 50% discount at retail sale immediately doubles every individual's potential purchasing power which means if you are making $30,000/yr. you now can potentially purchase $60,000/yr. worth of goods and services. Or you could spend $15,000 of your income while maintaining your current lifestyle and save $15,000/yr. that you can use to purchase $30,000 worth of whatever thing you so choose. Nice huh?

If you are a business-owner, the potential amount of available business revenue for your products and services has also just been immediately doubled. That's the definition of "good economic times" and the best opportunity for you the businessman to profit since...forever.

Note: Inflation occurring before retail sale is never a large percentage because competition is still alive between and within business models, and because the costs of technologically advanced fixed capital-intensive economies are very high. Thus, no enterprise can arbitrarily raise its prices by a high percentage because they would lose market share. Also, hyperinflation never occurs unless a series of prior disastrous circumstances happen first. So those who may have immediately closed their minds about this policy need to re-open them.

2) A universal dividend of $1000/mo. for everyone 18 years of age and older for life which paired with the 50% discount/rebate policy at retail sale guarantees every adult an annual purchasing power of $24,000.

3) A sliding scale policy of a 25-50% Gift/Debt Jubilee policy at the point of loan signing for all "big ticket" items, with the 50% debt jubilee being for ecologically sane purchases. This means that if you purchase a $300k home its price is reduced to $150k at retail sale by the 50% Discount/Rebate and then to $75k at note signing. It also means a $50k electric vehicle would cost $25k at retail and $12.5k at note signing and $40k worth of solar panels would cost you $10k. Finance must serve and free humanity, not hold it back or even oppress it. It must also enable the wisdom and ability to act for the better

survival of the species and the survival of all other species and the planet. The green product aspect of the second 50% discount/debt jubilee policy enables us to finally and rapidly progress toward ecologically sane industrial policies that have gone nowhere for over 50 years.

The Full List of Policies, Structural Changes and Programs of Wisdomics-Gracenomics, and Their Beneficial Monetary Statistics and Economic Effects for Individuals and Enterprise

1) A $1000/mo. universal dividend at age 18 for life, that with the 50% discount/rebate policy in policy #3 gives every adult individual a guaranteed potential to purchase $24,000 worth of goods and services yearly and a two-adult family will have $48,000/yr. in potential purchasing power. One can opt out of this beneficial policy if you consider it against your principles, but if you do, you cannot opt back into receiving it for 5 years.

2) A 50% discount to the consumer at retail sale on virtually all consumer items and a rebate of the entirety of that discount back to the enterprise giving it to their

customers/consumers by the monetary authority that creates all new money.

Note: Both the universal dividend and 50% discount/rebate policies would be guaranteed. There would not be any chance that the "rug could be pulled out from underneath" the security and paradigm changing potential of the synergistic effects of combining these two policies.

3) A sliding scale 25-50% Gift/Debt Jubilee policy at the point of loan signing for "big ticket items" like homes, automobiles, furnishings, solar power systems and any other high-cost green consumer products.

As an addendum to the 50% Gift/Debt Jubilee policy students can re-finance their student debt and receive a 50% reduction in the balance.

4) An Indexing of the discount percentage to any statistical monthly inflation Even if the yearly rate of inflation continues to be 1-3% then the discount/rebate percentage automatically will become 51-53%.

Yearly inflation has historically been a smallish single digit percentage. The primary reason for this is the costs of high-tech capital-intensive economic systems inhibits large increases in price. Thus, a big increase in price would enable competitors to capture your market share. The 50% discount at retail sale will thus abolish price and asset inflation forever.

5) A tax rate of 0% for yearly income up to $24,000 if filing individually and $48,000 if filing jointly. A tax rate of 2% for income from $48,001 to $100,000. A tax rate of 5% for income of $100,001-$250,000. A tax rate of 7% for income of $250,001-$1,000,000. A tax rate of 10% on income of $1,000,001-5,000,000. A tax rate of 12% on income of $5,000,001-$10,000,000. A tax rate of 15% on income of $10,000,001-$20,000,000. A tax rate of 20% on income of $20,000,001 and up

unless 25% of your income is given to a list of agreed upon causes/charities one does not have control over, then the tax rate is 0%

Corporate taxes will also be cut.

There will be a 1% tax of 25% of gross corporate income post accounting of legitimate deductions even if according to legitimate exemptions you owe no taxes.

6) Reduction of **Discount Percentage Sliding Scale According to Annual Personal Income**
$0-250,000
0%

$250,001-500,000   10%

$500,001-750,000
    20%

$750,001-1,000,000
    30%

$1,000,001-2,000,000   40%

$2,000,001-and up
    49%

7) A thorough review of all tax exemptions, and of the rationale for all cost accounting expensing. Accounting control fraud will not be allowed to game a truly benevolent

system and the sovereign and ethical right of government to tax.

8) Private Finance will be able to create money in Wisdomics-Gracenomics...if they abide by all the rules of the new paradigm program. If they don't, they will be severely taxed and lose the considerable benefits afforded them like for instance the 25-50% Gift/Debt Jubilee in policy #3 where they would receive 50% of the total note's interest up front that they can treat as profit in exchange for reducing the note by 50% to the consumer. Private for-profit finance's money creating powers and its dominating monopolistic

paradigm of Debt Only as the sole form and vehicle for the creation and distribution of money are both an unnecessary cost burden on the legitimate economic/productive process and a foolish ignoring of Lord Acton's dictum that power corrupts, and absolute power corrupts absolutely. After over 5000 years it is way overdue for the new paradigm of Abundantly Direct and Reciprocal Monetary Gifting to become the new reality. The gracious nature of the new paradigm finally breaks the spell of the old.

9) A push for the new monetary paradigm to become a fourth branch of government with constitutionally

arm's length separation from the other three branches. Its policy mandates will be the various monetary policies described here. That, and the unitary ethical guidance by the aspects of the natural philosophical concept of grace will keep it in the service of humanity, not its domination.

It cannot be stressed enough that a private for-profit banking and financial system with monopolistic control of the most powerful factor in the entire economy, namely the creation of money/credit, and only in the paradigmatic form of debt is the deepest economic problem that we currently face. However, a private Banking and financial system could be integrated into the Debt Only system and still profit if it aligns and abides by the new paradigm concept and its policies of monetary grace as in gifting. And making sure the natural philosophical and ethical concept of grace as in love in action and the gracious policies of Wisdomics-Gracenomics are not altered by enshrining them in a constitutionally separate branch of government is the best way to keep the economy guided by that concept.

10) A policy combination of either

A) a 30/hr. per week job guarantee for those having some difficulty in finding purpose and personal comfort without having a job, or

B) an option of 30 paid hours per week for any legitimate and constructive self-chosen personally purposeful activities.

In other words, anyone having trouble feeling lack of purpose has two options to help them find self-satisfying purpose. Employment is a much smaller subset of all positive and constructive human purposes, and acculturating purpose is the route to life-long happiness.

Instead of "the reserve army of the unemployed" a national job guarantee could create an army of tree planters, hemp farmers and other ecologically sane mega clean-up and re-cycling projects.

11) In the spirit of and the continuing pursuit of the Good, a National Economic Wisdom Council of philosophers, businessmen and scientists will be created to analyze the concept behind the new paradigm, the natural philosophical concept of grace, and consider the best and most effective ways to acculturate it into the economy and society. This must not be confused with religiosity, but rather as its title shows, simply wisdom.

Wisdom is ending the excessive, de-stabilizing and destructive financialization of the economy where "the big killing" has become a speculative obsession, and price and asset inflation are the result. Wisdom is an economy where all businesses exist in a monetarily abundant profit-making system and abide by the philosophy and policies that continually create that reality while innovating, competing, and serving their customers. This is the wise way out of the financialized trap we are in, and the way home to prosperity for all. It is a system where all agree not to greedily speculate and/or arbitrarily inflate and instead pursue an ethic of grace as in classically productive, prosperous dynamic balance.

12) The present pharmaceutical and health insurance industries and the stock and commodities corporations must also seriously heed the new paradigm of monetary gifting, its regulatory means of preventing price and asset inflation and its ethical implications, or they risk replacement by corporations that will heed them.

In the meantime, destructive speculation and arbitrary price inflation will not be allowed. Select leveraged speculation itself will be allowed on actual economic/productive processes, but it must and will align with both the new paradigm concept of grace and the classical economic virtues of increasing competition, innovation, thrift, and ecological sanity.

13) Institutionalize the Department of Competition, Innovation, Boycotting and The Public's Bully Pulpit that will be keen to break up monopolistic tendencies in commerce, and fund competitors to them if they resist the dynamic and ethical balance of policies based on the philosophical concept of grace/graciousness.

Initial attempts to game, de-stabilize and/or undue the paradigm changing policies of Wisdomics-Gracenomics by commercial entities arbitrarily raising their prices despite the cost savings and increased potential business revenue it brings to them will be taxed at much higher rates than usual, and they will be individually and publicly called out for their anti-social and greedy actions thus risking loss of good will which is the most precious commodity any business can possess. Repeated abuses will result in the organization of boycotts of their products and/or services and finally loss of the discount/rebate privilege if they persist in their arbitrary price raising. Two of the unified aspects of the natural philosophical concept of grace are benevolence and righteously sovereign willingness and ability to act against unethical behavior.

14) Wisdomics-Gracenomics embraces every possible rationally workable program, product and policy that will make more likely the sanity of ecologically sustainable production, consumption and energy usage. With the end of inflation and individual monetary scarcity resolved by its twin policies of a universal dividend and a 50% discount/rebate at retail sale, and with the end of private money creation no necessary environmental project will ever be "too expensive" again, and all manner of ecologically sane actions can be accomplished including:

l) Robust domestic economies instead of hollowed out ones with energy intensive and unnecessarily expensive global supply chains

II) With price deflation beneficially integrated into profit making systems via the twin 50% discount/rebate policies, a guaranteed reasonable income level via the $1000/mo. universal dividend and a job guarantee we will not have to worry about either inflation or unemployment and so rapid national re-industrialization in the most high-tech, productively efficient and ecologically sane means possible could begin immediately

III) Complete infrastructure upgrade and re-fit to meet the highest energy and pollution standards

IV) Doubling income does not necessarily equate with doubling consumption or economic through put, however we should still strive diligently to find innovative economic regulations and engineering strategies to guide consumption toward prudence as it is both a cardinal personal virtue, a systemic economic one and ecologically sane as well. Saving and investing under the directly distributive and inflation ending policies of Wisdomics-Gracenomics will no longer be a de-stabilizing macro-economic vice, and I suspect that the vast majority of people will quickly adapt to abundance with that prudent economic strategy, that is, saving, especially for big ticket items and experiences that will not stress the environment. The wisdom of having an economy based on the dynamic balance of the concept of grace should have wide beneficial cultural effects and we should welcome that as opposed to the unbalanced emotional and ecological consequences of wealth and conspicuous consumption that the current monetary and economic struggle too often evokes. To that end a policy of a sliding scale of required investment of gifted money in 5-6% eco-bonds will be implemented. A gift of investment is still a gift:

$0-$24,000
10%

$24k+-$100k
25%

100k+-$500k
50%

$500k+-$1000k
75%

$1000k and up
100%

V) Unlimited availability of financing for the best ecological research, innovations and their implementations. Wisdom and graciously wise actions toward planetary sustainability are, by definition, the ultimate ecological ethic, and the policies, structural changes, and regulations of

Wisdomics-Gracenomics will be exactly aligned with that effort. This will mean that while keeping competition, innovation and the profit motive preferred and always available, the hastened trend toward sustainability will still be the ruling consideration, and profit-making enterprise will ultimately bow to that most sane understanding. Human and ecological survival is not an option, it is a commandment of Wisdom.

Finally, the biggest and most essential ecological program is undoubtedly the off-planeting and/or under-planeting of much of production either in high earth orbit or on the moon which, while being the epitome of a massive project, cannot and should not be dismissed. And when affordability is no longer a financial consideration with Wisdomics-Gracenomics...full speed ahead!

15) Introducing The New Concept of GDP:

Grace-Evoking Domestic Product

Every policy, incentive, dis-incentive, tool like accounting etc. needs to be imbedded in/linked to everyday living in ways that elicit an aspect or aspects of the natural philosophical concept/experience of grace as in love/better survival...in action.

For instance: 50% Discount/Rebate policy at retail sale. Gratitude for a gift of price.

Same for my 50% Gift/Debt jubilee policy at point of loan signing 50% required investment of individually gifted money into solving the energy, ecological, super organism problems into 5-6% eco-bonds. Gifting begets gratitude and gratifying sense of helpfulness and positive purpose.

Any profit a business invests in such above bonds or in selected research and development of eco-projects/grace evoking cultural thrusts (like organic/regenerative farming, permaculture, regenerative medicine, new CCC etc. etc.) will be matched with eco-bonds in the business' name/account by the money system. Gifting begets gratitude, gratifying sense of helpfulness, positive purpose and increased abundance of cultural experience of grace in everyday life.

I'm sure there are many other ways and opportunities to evoke the aspects of grace in our everyday activities and we must search for and implement them. Again, this can obviously be done in the economy and money system but let us apply the benefits of grace in all our systems. This is the deeper message of this book.

16) A non-inflationary, stable, and abundantly beneficial directly distributive fiat money system integrated into profit making economic systems will enable a dramatic reduction in individual and corporate taxation. (see policy #6)

Re-distributive transfer taxation for welfare, unemployment insurance and social security will virtually end because with the universal dividend, twin 50% discount/rebate policies and the job guarantee policies such taxation will be redundant and no longer needed.

Furthermore, individual, and corporate income taxation for 99% of the populace could be reduced. There will be fewer deductions and appropriate penalties for cheating and avoiding taxes. The state needs to establish the reality of its sovereignty and yet be both non-wasteful and benevolent in its intents and policies. Benevolence and sovereignty are both aspects of the ultimate integrative natural philosophical concept of grace after all.

17) A cooperative effort by the helping professions, the clergy and the government with public service announcements like the ones used to reduce smoking should be undertaken to help positively and constructively acculturate the general populace to leisure, to find

other constructive purposes in addition to employment, to build stronger communities, to reform business practices and align the culture toward ecological sanity throughout the land.

18) Revenue garnered by arbitrary price rises made by enterprise despite the tremendous cost savings of reduced and eliminated taxes and the benefits of more than doubling of demand for their products and services will be taxed at a rate of 100%. Conversely tax reductions will be awarded to businesses that do compete on price.

Loss of rebate privileges will also be enforced if chronic gaming of the new paradigm is committed.

If commercial economic agents and individuals cannot see the personal and economic benefits of abiding by the beatific chains of an ethic of monetary grace as in gifting, hopefully corrective measures will aid them in attaining that insight.

The irony of the 50% discount/rebate policy and its related regulations is that they "compel" business models to accept the prosperously freeing doubling of potential business revenue they create or go out of business because if you don't "opt in" you must get 100% of your best competitive price while your competition who does opt in only has to get 50% of their price from the consumer. It also enables enterprise to cut their costs because of the elimination of transfer taxation. This makes it even more difficult for any enterprise to justify raising their prices because their costs are cut which enables greater profits. Finally, if you still raise your prices and your competition cuts their prices even more because of their cost savings.... how much market share are you likely to lose???

Irony is a signature of paradigm change, and of spirituality. All the signatures of the former are elucidated later in this book.

Choosing the beatifically "compelling" chains of the unitary ethic of grace is the ultimate wisdom and sanity.

19) In return for the more than doubling of available individual income and hence more than doubling business revenue with the dividend and discount policies, all enterprises will submit to a rigorous monthly accounting analysis of their books. Decreased costs can legitimately be made business profits, but given those cost savings, any arbitrary price increases without

actual total economic cost increases, figuring in and including the financial cost savings made possible by the non-profit national banking and financial system of Wisdomics-Gracenomics, will not be tolerated. If the new growth area of the economy is forensic accounting, so be it. An army of such accountants could only be a force for honesty, for continuing prosperity for all and for systemic stability.

20) A 12-month public service program for young people starting at age 16 and served either in 2-month intervals during summer vacation or with the option to serve the 12 months entirely for youth 18 and

older. This service will include needed employment in new infrastructure, programs for environmental studies, artistic and craft expression, and with a comparative study of the world's major wisdom traditions including the non-sectarian natural philosophical concept of grace and its healthy and beneficial aspects in all areas of life. It is time for humanity to leave its lingering adolescence and to mature into a culture of wisdom. The acculturation of wisdom should start as early as possible for every young person and hopefully will be embraced by everyone no matter their age.

21) The central bank in a paradigm of monetary grace will look askance at any large leveraging up for any speculative purposes, and any attempts to short the currency from domestic or foreign sources will immediately be considered "null and void" by our legal and political systems. Speculators in commodities markets will not be allowed excessively large leveraging, and if such markets do not abide by all regulations, new ones will undoubtedly be created that will so abide.

The central banking system will not encourage individuals or enterprise to borrow large amounts of money for speculative investment. In fact, along with the universal dividend, the twin discount/rebate policies at retail sale and loan signing, it will enable and encourage them to utilize savings to partially or completely purchase big ticket items. After all grace as in prudence/balance is a cardinal virtue both personally and economically.

Loans to business and for business start-ups will still have to be well considered to receive funds. Malinvestment will be discouraged.

And again, one of the primary goals of Wisdomics-Gracenomics, and of the publicly administered national banking/central banking system it will implement, is to hasten the end of expensive, far flung and potentially unstable supply chains and enable and encourage rapid re-industrialization of the country in the most technologically advanced, productively efficient and ecologically sane way possible.

The Specific Monetary Numbers for Both the Individual and For Enterprise

Students and anyone 18 years of age and older would have a lifetime universal dividend amounting to $24,000/yr. of guaranteed purchasing power ($1000/mo. x 2 with the 50% discount x 12) and so they could attend all but the most expensive colleges, be able to pay for tuition and room and board as they attended (which will also be discounted 50% as they are the retail product of college education) and not become saddled by huge debts upon graduation. With a part time job, they could have a more than comfortable lifestyle while attending as well.

A two adult household will have $48,000/yr. of guaranteed purchasing power.

For 2 adults with two $18,000/yr. jobs that is another $72,000/yr. ($36,000 +50 % discount = $72,000) or a total of $120,000/yr. of potential purchasing power.

With the 50% discount also extended to the point of note signing a $300k home would be reduced to $150k at retail sale and at note signing the remaining $150k would be disbursed to the home building corporation to make them whole on their total costs and price, and then the monetary authority would reduce the actual note by 50% reducing the cost to the buyer to $75k.

The difference between the two costs of those loans within the present paradigm and without Wisdomics-Gracenomics' policies would be: $300k house at 5% for 30 years would equal a monthly payment of $1610 plus insurance and taxes. With the policies of Wisdomics-Gracenomics a $75k house at 0% for a 10-year note would be a monthly payment of $625 plus insurance and taxes. That is almost a thousand dollars less per month and only a 10-year term instead of a 30-year mortgage/death contract.

With the universal dividend, the 50% discount/rebate policies at retail sale and the extension of the 50% discount at note signing for more expensive and ecologically sane consumer items and assets, the first true ownership economy will become a reality.

Everyone gets an account at the central bank and the debits and credits balance like any other commercial agent

When was the last time an economist or politicians of either stripe came up with a more beneficial set of policies for all agents individual and commercial, and that accomplishes the cardinal signature of genuine paradigm changes, namely complete inversion of old paradigm realities?

Short answer: Never.

Understanding the Nature of Paradigmatic Thinking and the Effects of New Paradigms

Paradigmatic thinking is the highest form of both the scientific and the holistic perspective and discipline of Wisdom. It tries to combine, refine, and show how to implement systemic policy in a better fashion out of dualistically opposed orthodoxies from which the new paradigm has emerged. Hence it is a thoroughly integrative genuine third-ness greater oneness.

Third-ness greater oneness has always been a signature of wisdom, and paradigmatic thinking is exactly that, the correct integration of both scientific and wisdom thinking.

As shown in the introduction there is an ascending scale of intellectual actions and ways to know where every level higher includes all the accurate and truthful ways of knowing below it. It goes from research/data gathering, to theory formation, to philosophy, to paradigmatic perception and understanding, and at the top what is referred to as a zeitgeist or ethic of the age. Most people and most scientists get stymied and stuck in the theory formation level and so get stuck in the obsessive contentiousness and complexities of dualities like capitalism versus socialism.

When one enters the philosophy level, hopefully they begin to consider all the aspects of the ideas on both sides of the duality in a consistent fashion and consider the ethical implications of each as well. This is the beginning of the truly integrative process and is above the necessary but mentally fragmenting process of science. Above the philosophy level is hopefully the identification of a single concept that fits within the body of knowledge under study and whose aspects also bring even higher understanding, workability and transformation. That is the definition of paradigmatic thinking. Unfortunately, this doesn't always happen usually because theorists and philosophers fail to recognize the signatures of imminent and accomplished historical paradigm changes which are their guideposts. These signatures will be enumerated and examined later in this book.

Again, a new paradigm is a single concept that describes and creates new realities within a new pattern. Thus, most old orthodoxies fall by the wayside with paradigm changes. This has been historically true with every paradigm change, or it wouldn't be a paradigm change. It's the nature of the beast and its mental and temporal effects.

Almost all critiques of a new paradigm have historically been mere insistence that we respect old paradigm realities when they have been replaced or transformed by the new one. This is no desire to suppress research or rational discourse, but the most important thing to consider is to assess whether, or not the claims for the new paradigm fulfill most or all of the signatures of historical paradigm changes. That is a new paradigm's truest test.

New paradigms often make what are considered significant realities and truths in the old paradigm relatively insignificant or irrelevant. That's because a new insight, which resulted in the awareness of the paradigm concept itself and its new resolving powers, has rendered them so.

Another important thing to be aware of regarding paradigms is that they include only the particles of truth and the highest workability's, applicability's and ethical considerations of apparently opposing perspectives. They integrate these factors in such a way that a separate and actual thirdness is the result. They are higher order levels of integrative thinking and awareness in the body of knowledge/area of human endeavor in which the paradigm applies, and that include all or most of the above essential factors.

In other words, paradigm changes are intellectually discriminating but simultaneously non-prejudicial mental and ethical combinations which establish both their scientific bona fides and their even deeper and more holistic claims to being wisdom insights.

Finally, old/current paradigms are habitually and so almost entirely unconsciously accepted norms. That is why it is so difficult for those analyzing an area needing a paradigm change to "think outside of the box" and so be able to completely visualize them.

How the Policy Suggestions of All of the Leading-Edge Economist's Reflect and Align with the Policies and the Concept Behind Wisdomics-Gracenomics and Yet Will Not Resolve Our Problems...Because They Haven't Recognized The Specific New Monetary Paradigm Concept

The natural philosophical concept behind Wisdomics-Gracenomics is grace as in abundant dynamic, interactive and integrative free flowingness.

What is the thing all cutting edge economists, economic theories and reforms like MMT, Steve Keen's

Minsky Financial Instability Hypothesis, Michael Hudson's financial parasitism and Ellen Brown's Public Banking suggest in their policies and want to see?

Answer: Creating the best amount of money in the economy and yet avoiding both recession and inflation. As these two results are the complete opposite of each other even the smartest and best intentioned reformists and their movements are in what is referred to as a "double bind".

The only thing they lack is an awareness of the specific new monetary paradigm concept and its best application points in the economy.

And a single policy of a 50% discount/rebate at retail sale that will solve both of those problems and more in one fell swoop.

Leading heterodox economists (unlike their currently dominant neo-classical colleagues) have indeed come back around from austerity as part of the answer, to correct if palliative policies that economists who preceded them have suggested before. Debt jubilees have been around since ancient history, UBI/Universal dividend was suggested by C. H. Douglas long before it became the rage recently, and his policy of a compensated retail discount which I have extended and innovated into a paradigm changing policy all by itself, would resolve the two deepest problems of modern economies that present theorists seek, but still have not figured out how to fix.

As I said all heterodox economists want to inject more money into the economy, but they are still unable to resolve the lingering problems of compulsive private debt build up and chronic price and asset inflation. Some claim that their theories will eliminate inflation, but they are on very shaky ground because money isn't the most basic and primary cause of "monetary" inflation. The truth is the most basic cause of inflation is the fetishized concept of the free market which in reality is an inevitably unstable dominance by the monetary and financial paradigm of Debt Only as the sole form and vehicle for the creation and distribution of money. The 50% discount/rebate policy terminally deals with inflation by inverting it into beneficial price and asset deflation.

The 50% discount/rebate policy is the exact expression of the new paradigm of Abundantly Direct and Reciprocal Monetary Gifting. It will empirically, temporally, continually, and so scientifically, resolve these two problems in dynamically ongoing fashion, and resolve other burdens born by both individuals and enterprise that the heterodox aren't even thinking can be or need to be fixed.

The three policies of a $1000/mo. universal dividend, a 50% discount/rebate at retail sale and 25-50% Gift/Debt Jubilee at the point of loan signing together resolve the problems of the continual build-up of debt service costs, individual monetary scarcity, and price and asset inflation.

The Signatures of Imminent and Accomplished Paradigm Change and Other Historical Facts Regarding Them

SIGNATURES OF IMMINENT PARADIGM CHANGE:

I. Increasing Rigidity and Stubborn Unworkability of Orthodoxies in the Area to Which A Paradigm Applies

Ptolemaic terra-centrism (that the earth was the center of the cosmos and the sun and other heavenly bodies revolved around it) was the ruling cosmological idea for centuries, and while tweaking it had improved the anomalies in the tracking of heavenly bodies they were never actually resolved. For a variety of reasons the orthodoxies surrounding it terra-centrism became very resistant to change.

Today neo-liberal general equilibrium theory is the ruling macro-economic ideology and has resisted change even though more than a decade later we are still suffering the negative effects of the GFC ("The Great Financial Crisis") of 2008 which its advocates did not foresee. And, despite the fact that its most basic assumptions have been thoroughly de-bunked, it remains the major viewpoint in economic theory. This is a sure sign that a new paradigm is needed.

II. Iconoclasm, But Fear of Invalidation

Because old paradigms are habitual patterns they resist deep and consequential change. They build up unresolved problems that intellectuals and scientists rail against, and in so doing begin to break the image of the old paradigm. I've seen this necessary process take place for over 15 years since the GFC, and yet after the first couple of years I got tired of the continual re-gurgitation of the correct critiques and decided that the next step of identifying the single concept that produces an entirely new pattern of realities was necessary. That was the genesis of Wisdomics-Gracenomics.

Iconoclasm is a good intellectual tool, but it is not generally up to paradigm perception because dissecting an economy's many complexities does not necessarily lend itself to the entire pattern's solutions. That requires things like an integrative attitude toward the particles of truth existing in opposing perspectives, and a willingness and ability to consider the possibility of using illogic as a means of leaving the mindset of the current paradigm.

Unfortunately, these are extremely rare intellectual qualities, especially by the current neo-classical "authorities" who usually have ego involvement with the old paradigm, and even with the iconoclastic, who despite wanting to change the present paradigm still reside in the current paradigm for inquiry. That paradigm is Science as the only legitimate means of inquiry. Hence, they often become very cautious about being wrong out of a fear of risking their reputations.

III. Authoritarianism

Authoritarianism always sees an uptick if not a parabolic rise under the stressful and uncertain circumstances of an old paradigm gone on too long. And this is exactly what we are seeing in our current political and social climate today. The strong man political temptation has occurred so many times throughout history when the stress of unresolved problems have piled up, and the disastrous consequences that have always followed from it are so apparent it's a wonder it isn't a glaring red light that everyone can agree is a wrong turn.

Authoritarianism is inevitably polarizing and ultimately disintegrative which is exactly the opposite of what is presently needed in the economy, finance and our money system, namely a paradigm changing *integration* of only the truths, workability's, applicability's and highest ethical considerations in opposing perspectives.

IV. Intellectual Uncertainty, Obsession with Complexity and Chaos

Intellectual uncertainty is part and parcel of the necessary and inevitable process of iconoclasm. However, to get beyond iconoclasm, it is necessary to envision a new paradigm.

Other than Wisdomics-Gracenomics there is virtually no search for the single concept that defines and creates the new pattern, the new monetary and financial paradigm.

Virtually all theorists except myself are to one degree or another still stuck in the argumentation and ultimately confusing and chaotic effects of the problem...instead of looking for the actual solution which is a new pattern, a new vision that resolves. All these theorists are extremely erudite and well intentioned, but they are also obsessively stuck in the complexities of economic theory....and we're going nowhere but toward more theoretical chaos as a result.

The new paradigm, its philosophy and its policies has been discovered in Wisdomics-Gracenomics. We need to take the advice of a man who was known for his innovative thinking and advocacy of paradigm change R. Buckminster Fuller:

"You never change things by fighting the existing reality.
To change something, build a new model that makes the existing model obsolete."

V. A Change From Unwillingness, to Willingness to Consider Complete Conceptual Opposition

Every new paradigm is conceptually oppositional in significant ways from the old/current one.

The cardinal signature of imminent paradigm change, in fact the final consideration that enables paradigm change to occur in one's mind, has always been the willingness to consider complete conceptual opposition to current orthodoxy and to the current paradigm. It is always apparently illogical and an absurdity to consider a new paradigm. It is so much easier and safer to tweak theory, to advocate for reforms or even to merely destroy the image of the old paradigm, but to make it to the other side you've got to find the single oppositional concept that defines the new paradigm, and then take that single concept and test it to confirm that it also fits within the present legitimate structures existing within the old pattern while also creating the new one.

As it was with nomadic hunting and gathering to homesteading, agriculture and the rise of city states and nations, so it will be with Debt Only as the sole form and vehicle for the creation and distribution of new money to its oppositional concept of Direct and Reciprocal Monetary Gifting.

Illogic can be a break down, or a breakthrough. The oppositional concept of the new paradigm of Monetary Gifting is of the latter variety.

And if we don't consider complete conceptual opposition and do not choose to act, we will get the chaos of continuing disintegration.

VI. Resentment and Revolt by the Polis and General Break Down

Trumpism, Brexit, Gilets Jaunes/Yellow Vests, "Fourth Turnings" are all signs of the times. The signs that we must integrate the truths, workability's, applicability's, and highest ethical considerations in opposing perspectives...or inevitably face chaos and breakdown.

And consider this: historically a general breakdown always results in war, thorough disruption and destruction of normal existence, and today with our extremely deadly weaponry that means the death of multiple millions of innocents….and that quite likely means YOU and YOUR family. You…dead. Your family…dead. Please think about that briefly, and do the logically survival decision…to DO SOMETHING EFFECTIVE ABOUT IT. Like creating a mass movement to get the new paradigm implemented.

Mere fear mongering is the work of demagogues. However, rational consideration of oft observed historical trends, honest awareness of the current situation and then acting in a forthright way that integrates truths and brings better survival….is wisdom.

Integration of truths is the answer. Failing to recognize the urgent necessity to fight for and accomplish such an integration is the height of ignorance and apathy.

Please save yourself and your family from the almost inevitable disaster that failing to accomplish a new paradigm in economics and the money system will result in, by helping me begin the mass movement that can rapidly implement that new paradigm.

SIGNATURES OF ACCOMPLISHED PARADIGM CHANGE:

1) The Discovery of a New Tool and/or Insight, or the Re-Discovery of an Old Tool or Insight

Note: This is basically a repetition of the prior information regarding retail sale, but it is still very important as it also shows that realizing the significance of a direct and reciprocal monetary policy at retail sale is an accomplished aspect of the new monetary, economic and financial paradigm. In fact, the 50% discount/rebate policy at retail sale is the very expression of the new paradigm concept itself.

The recognition that the point of retail sale is the single macro-economic point in the entire economic process is actually a new macro-economic insight. Why? Because macro-economics is about aggregates and aggregative effects, and the fact that everyone directly or indirectly participates in retail sale means it will have universal effect. And no one else besides me seems to presently recognize this.

Thank you, Nobel Prize Committee. ☐

No more perfect example of how economists are distracted by abstraction and hence blinded to the significances to be found in the normal present time operations of the everyday economy can be illustrated by this fact. It has been there a billion times a day for them to see, but they have never looked at it and so missed the incredible economic and monetary insights and problem resolution potentials to be found there.

The point of retail sale is also, very significantly, the terminal ending point for the entire economic/productive process for every consumer item or service. In other words, it is the point where production becomes consumption which means no other (legitimate) economic/productive factor can change or add to the costs of a sale at retail, and that exposes private for-profit money creation as an entirely exterior cost increasing parasite. This fact, so long unperceived and allowed to go on, is another one of the major new insights of the new paradigm. But hold on, I've even innovated a policy that effectively, and even beneficially, integrates private finance back into the legitimate economic process.

Nobel Prize. No, better a mass movement and, right along with it, the greatest opportunity to raise the general psychological experience mankind has ever created by making the everyday universally participated in infrastructure of participating in the economy also an opportunity to self-actualize gratitude. Visualize it.

But I digress. How many of you have ever gone to a grocery store, bought items worth $100, and when you got home the retailer called you and said, "Oops, sorry, the front office just got the report that inflation has gone up by 30% so we need to have another $30 for those items. Never. Because when you've paid the full price at final retail sale that is where and when production has become consumption. It is said possession is 90% of the law, and I guarantee you possession as in consumption is 99.99% of the economic process.

Because retail sale is indeed the terminal ending and summing points of production, it must also be, by definition, the terminal expression point for all forms of inflation. Hence a discount/rebate policy of 50% at retail sale will not only eliminate any possibility of inflation which almost never exceeds a small single digit percentage, it will painlessly and beneficially integrate price deflation into profit making economic systems.

And that is a paradigm changing effect all by itself.

An additional insight is the recognition that the most basic cause of inflation is not money itself, but rather a scarcity of total income in ratio to total costs and the lack of a better, more rational and beneficial alternative for commercial agents who, existing in that system of enforced scarcity of individual income, are then strongly incentivized to raise their prices when they see more money coming into the system...in order to hopefully garner more business revenue. That is just another double bind...that the policies of Wisdomics-Gracenomics resolves.

This is one of the key insights that opens one's mind to the new paradigm:

Money itself is at best a tertiary cause of inflation.

1a) The current financial paradigm of Debt Only dominates virtually every enterprise and almost everyone in the economy. Another new insight is that the new paradigm can strategically use the same method that private finance uses to create upwards of 95% of all our new money, namely the accounting operations of equal debits and credits that sum to zero, to resolve our economic problems because accounting is probably the most temporal reality anchoring discipline man has ever invented. So if we can use accounting to anchor the reality that all new money can only be created and distributed as debt, then we can also anchor and strategically integrate the problem resolving new monetary paradigm reality of Gifting into the economy…BY UTILIZING THE SAME METHOD.

The new insight of a direct and reciprocal monetary gifting policy at the point of retail sale will free everyone and implement the new paradigm.

> 2) Generally Increased Abundance

Generally increased abundance was what sealed the paradigm change from Hunting and Gathering to

Agriculture. It was also the case with the increased speed and productive level of communication with the Gutenberg Press, the proliferation of information with Cybernation and the expansion of scientific knowledge of the universe with the Copernican cosmological paradigm change.

The increased abundance of individual purchasing power and business revenue in the new paradigm perfectly reflect this major signature of paradigm change. And of course, the fact that abundance is an aspect of the natural philosophical concept of grace reinforces the idea that it is indeed the concept BEHIND the new monetary paradigm.

The only way to begin to overcome the tyranny of monetary scarcity and the false orthodoxy that increasing the money supply will inevitably lead to inflation is to implement the new paradigm of Abundantly Direct and Reciprocal Monetary Grace As In Gifting at the point of retail sale.

I. Clarity, New Vision, Transformation and Re-Integration of All But the Most Misaligned Structures of the Old Paradigm

Clarity, a new vision, transformation of our view of the physical universe, of our centralized position in the universe and a more accurate scientific viewpoint were the effects of the Copernican Cosmological paradigm change. Eventually the Catholic Church was forced to acknowledge this and accept that their conflation of the centralized supremacy of God with the position of the earth was not physically accurate and thus re-integrated that viewpoint accordingly.

Every paradigm change is, by definition, a clarifying, transformative and re-integrating new vision and event.

When economists and the individual recognize that the 50% discount/rebate policy at the point of retail sale is both the abundance bringing event and the very expression of the new monetary, financial and economic paradigm itself I am confident that it will be both a clarifying moment and one of the greatest leaps forward for homo sapiens in the entire history of human civilization.

II. The Resolution of Obsessive Dualistic Contention, Complete Inversion of Present Realities and Hence A True Integrative Thirdness Greater Oneness

If willingness to consider conceptual opposition is the cardinal signature of imminent paradigm change, then complete inversion of individual and systemic reality is the same for accomplished paradigm change.

More government spending? Good idea, but just a reform. UBI? Good idea, but just a first step. "A modern debt jubilee"? A very good idea, but a one-off static policy. MMT? A well-considered body of monetary thought and the correct mechanics of fiat money creation, but not a new paradigm. Disequilibrium and Financial Instability Theory? Accurate observations regarding the old/current paradigm, but not a program of the new paradigm.

Financial Parasitism? Spot on, but the ancients used debt jubilees to periodically reset the system, and yet the monopolistic paradigm of Debt Only never changed and so it went right back to being a destabilizing parasite that oppressed everyone. We must be smarter than the ancients.

A true integration of only the truths, only the highest workability's, the highest applicability's and highest ethical considerations of capitalist and socialist economics would be neither capitalism nor socialism, but the thirdness greater oneness of a graciously abundant profit-making system for all via a direct and reciprocal distributive paradigm of monetary gifting being integrated into the debt-based system.

Let's have all the correct ideas and policies that will completely invert the old realities and create a true thirdness greater oneness that is the accomplishment of a paradigm change. In other words, let's have Wisdomics-Gracenomics.

III. Simplicity of Operation of The Paradigm Change Itself and The Cutting Through and/or Undoing of Complexity and Former Orthodoxy

The basic operations/actions of a new paradigm are always very simple themselves.

Hunting and Gathering societies simply stopped seemingly enforced moving around and stayed in place. They stopped chasing game to survive and confined and bred them to eat and profit from. In other words, they did the opposite of what they were doing before because it increased their survival.

The Reformation was simply the ending of a monopoly power. That power was the ending of an arbitrary and indirect rule regarding absolution/resolution of the problem of sin only via the sacraments of the Roman Catholic Church, and the realization that one could have a direct and reciprocal relationship with God instead.

The Copernican cosmological paradigm change was simply the inversion of the positions of the earth and the sun. That inversion was also a transformation in the mind of mankind, a complete inversion of assumed obvious, necessary and unchangeable realities, an increase in scientific knowledge and a cutting through and undoing of complexities and orthodoxies that had built up around the former geo-centric paradigm.

The new paradigm of monetary gifting is simply the opposite of the current paradigm of Debt Only.

Monetary gifting ends the monopoly power of private banking's credit creation and the equally monopoly paradigm of Debt Only as the sole form and vehicle for the creation and distribution of money. It is the realization that a direct and reciprocal monetary and price policy at retail sale enables all agents to better accomplish and partake in the supreme purposes of economics, namely production, profit, sale and hence consumption.

Direct and reciprocal monetary gifting simply inverts and transforms the individual and systemic monetary realities of scarcity and austerity into abundance for all. It also inverts the assumed obvious, necessary and unchangeable realities that injecting more money into the economy will result in inflation and shows how the timely and strategic injection of more money at retail sale enables the actual solution to the problem of inflation. It increases our knowledge of the economic process and the significances of the point of retail sale and cuts through and undoes many of the economic complexities and orthodoxies that have built up around the paradigm of Debt Only.

IV. Generalized Psychological Relief from Stress, A Resultant Joy and Renewed Cooperative Spirit, and If the Paradigm change Occurs in an Area of Widespread and Chronic Effect and Long Time Enforced Domination By the Old Paradigm, the Resulting Integration of the New Paradigm Has "Knock On" Positive Effects in Numerous Other Bodies of Knowledge/Areas of Human Endeavor

The paradigm of Debt Only has been enforced for the entire history of human civilization, and that monopolistic idea has parasitically intertwined itself into the greater part of the time, effort and attention of nearly everyone's life via the economy that it dominates. But what if that was ended by the abundant monetary policies of Wisdomics-Gracenomics? What other areas of our lives could be better as a result?

Political

Our two-party political system has been obsessively contending with each other for a hundred years about whether to and how best to regulate finance and make the economy become and remain stable for all. Economic and monetary misconceptions and demagoguery have been rampant on both sides and we had a crisis a little over 15 years ago. We're in a slow-motion palliative recovery from the debt build up created in the run up to that crisis and theoretically only a few policy tweaks have resulted from all the correct critiques of the ruling economic ideology. With the policies of Wisdomics-Gracenomics finally resolving the deepest and most chronic problems of the economy politicians on both sides of the aisle will have to "give up the ghost" of their pet capitalist and socialist tweaks and get on with each other implementing the rest of the regulatory program of the profit-making system of direct monetary distributism known as Wisdomics-Gracenomics. The policies of Wisdomics-Gracenomics integrate the self-interests of traditionally opposed political perspectives. How pleasant would actual progress and cooperation between politicians be? And how much more social cohesion might we have if all the demagoguing and negativity of recent years finally ended?

Social

As per above with our politics, the social environment would undoubtedly become vastly less contentious with the ending of individual income scarcity and the end of inflation. People will have more time, more inclination to strengthen their family and social lives and more money to fill their lives with more meaningful and rewarding activities. The job guarantee/self-chosen meaningful purposes and the cooperative effort between the clergy, the helping professions and the government planks of Wisdomics-Gracenomics are intended to help promote social cohesion and acculturate us to the abundance and increased leisure time made available by its monetary policies.

We can either do this now or we can foolishly ignore such measures until the disruptive force of artificial intelligence eliminates 35-40% of current employment and we're confronted with a huge nationwide social-psychological problem without the forward-thinking policies of Wisdomics-Gracenomics. Which one of those two alternatives looks better and more rational to you?

Psychological

What if you could go to college, pay your tuition out of your pocket, have a decent lifestyle in the process and not have $50-75,000 of debt to weigh you down after you graduated? How wonderful a vision is that, and would it give you more hope and energy going forward for the next 60-70 years?

What if there was more than twice as much individual income and business revenue available to you than there ever was for the last several hundred years? Would that motivate you to work harder, and would the anxieties and difficulties of running a business be at the very least a little less intense?

What if there was a lot more money to build better schools, to increase and expand the local infrastructure in your community and to support local businesses like there was in the hay day of the middle class in the fifties and sixties? Would that make for a stronger, better, happier nation from the grassroots upward?

Money doesn't make you happy, but abundant money can facilitate so many things that can and will make your life better and fuller, and a full life is the definition of a happy life.

The stress imposed by the money system's monopolistic paradigm of Debt Only increasingly hangs around the necks of nearly all of us. Lifting that burden with permanent monetary abundance, stable economic prosperity and systemic free flowingness would probably enable the greatest increase in confidence, hope, joy and human purposefulness since the paradigm change from Hunting and Gathering to Agriculture, Homesteading and Urbanization.

Please visualize these political, social and psychological benefits made manifest by the policies of Wisdomics-Gracenomics….and join me in the mass movement to get them implemented.

V. Primacy of the New Paradigm

Primacy of the new paradigm is another signature of accomplished paradigm change. When we went from Nomadic Hunting and Gathering to Homesteading and Agriculture, we never went back to the primacy of nomadic life again. When the Gutenberg Press made communication abundant, we never went back to the time-consuming primacy of hand-written Bibles and other forms of communication.

The primacy of the new paradigm won't mean there won't be loans, it won't even mean that private finance will be completely eliminated, but it will mean there will be the new primacy of an abundant economy based on monetary grace as in gifting for all...and that is enabling of better survival and accomplishment of the general Good.

VI. The Historically Verifiable and Extremely Important Fact That: Everything Adapts to A New Paradigm...Not the Other Way Around.

This is the biggest reason why this book does not have to be five hundred or a thousand pages long, filled with a bunch of mathematical equations that make everyone's eyes glaze over and a bunch of citations of authorities whose mindset and conclusions remain largely within the old paradigm.

A new paradigm qualitatively creates an entirely new pattern but leaves all but the most misaligned structures and basic operations virtually unchanged. In other words investment will still be based on the traditional research and market factors to be considered, private banking will still exist but its dominance of virtually everyone and every other business model will end. Better to have a single unitary system guided by the unimpeachable ethical concept of grace as in monetary gifting and its policies...rather than trying to herd a bunch of greed crazed rogue corporate entities toward the common good.

When we viewed the heavens with the telescope and discovered that the earth revolved around the sun not the other way around, we never went back to the prior perspective.

When the Gutenberg Press made abundant machine produced communications possible, I'm sure there were people who said, "Oh my god, you're going to put all of the scribes and monks out of work!", but everything and everybody adapted to the new paradigm...not the other way around.

And when Abundantly Direct and Reciprocal Monetary Gifting is recognized as the new monetary, financial and economic paradigm we'll never go back to Debt Only as the sole means and vehicle for the creation and distribution of money....and everything in the money system, economics and banking will adapt to that new paradigm...not the other way around.

So, when someone critiques this book because it is "just a polemic", "it doesn't enumerate how every jot and tittle of economics will be addressed", "it's too radical", or it doesn't fit their favorite, orthodox and mere theory, blah, blah, blah…just ignore it…because everything in the area of a new paradigm adapts to the new paradigm. Nearly all of the orthodox pundits and theorists that are still in the mindset of the old paradigm will be of little or no consequence and their viewpoints will either disappear or be integrated into the greater truth and the greater good, if the new paradigm has all of the signatures it should have and resolves the old paradigm's lingering problems…as I've shown in the last three sections of this book.

Of course, all of the people and structures that own and control or believe in the current old paradigm system are going to try to find as many nit-picking critiques of the new paradigm as they can...that's an almost natural reaction, but an authentic new paradigm sweeps all of those objections aside. That's how truly powerful and beneficial a new paradigm is.

All we really need to do is focus on helping others to visualize the new paradigm and stopping any of the unethical attempts to game or undo the new paradigm that the worst of the old paradigm crowd will undoubtedly try. Like for instance the private banks leveraging up speculators to short the currency.

That's why part of the program of Wisdomics-Gracenomics prohibits such actions by declaring them "null and void" even before they are attempted.

We need to understand that most present structures and operations will remain in place. The incredible benefits of the universal dividend and 50% discount/rebate policies will become apparent immediately, and the system will progress in permanent ways that insures we'll never go back to the inhumane dominance, destructive tendencies and systemic instability that was the old paradigm of Debt Only.

I understand some of this is anathema to the incremental inclinations of the scientific mindset that nearly everyone is habituated to, and I hasten to add that I am four-square for science itself...it's just that a paradigm change is a pattern change NOT just a new datum, a new theory or even a new philosophy. A paradigm change is an utterly basic and earth moving occurrence. So much so that there is no going back to the old paradigm way of thinking. It doesn't mean that aspects and structures of the old paradigm completely disappear, but the primacy will have shifted from the old to the new paradigm and the beneficial aspects of the new one will be so obvious that, as I showed in the preceding sections , historically we've never gone back to the dominating primacy and problematic nature of the old paradigm.

VII. The Dynamic Balance and The Ecological Sanity of Wisdomics-Gracenomics

The new monetary and financial paradigm will abolish forever the "too expensive" label for necessary and stabilizing infrastructure, and for ecologically sustainable projects. Hope for a long and more natural future for all humans, for all other species and for the planet will become a much more achievable goal. One of the aspects of the natural philosophical concept of grace is fully integrative, dynamic and ongoing balance. That is the exact mindset of both Wisdomics-Gracenomics and the body of knowledge known as ecology.

As the wisdom adage that "As a man thinketh, so is he" is obviously and logically correct, so that mindset will take root in ourselves and we will be able to proceed toward survival instead of the chaos and the suicidal result of ecological collapse. Again, the twin 50% discount/rebate, 50%

discount/debt jubilee policies will enable us to rapidly proceed toward ecological sanity instead of risking the folly of denial and doing nothing…which is what we have done about confronting climate change for the last 50 years.

So, let us end the reign of finance's dominating monopolistic paradigm of Debt Only, finally integrate the highest political, social and psychological intentions and enable ecological sanity to be pursued.

With such positive and progressive things resulting from the new paradigm of Abundantly Direct and Reciprocal Monetary Gifting mankind can begin to grow into its actual species designation of homo sapiens, i.e. wise and discerning man...instead of being forced to remain in the dead-end failed experiment of homo economicus that the paradigm of Debt Only has oppressed and herded us into for the last 5000 years.

VIII. The Concept of A Mega-Paradigm Change

This is a new idea. An authentic paradigm change is always transformational to the specific body of knowledge it applies to, but a mega-paradigm change directly, personally and continuously affects everyone's life in many ways including in areas not directly applicable to the main body of knowledge it applies to.

The Copernican Cosmological paradigm change changed astronomy forever, but our lives weren't continuously changed by it, and it did little or nothing to directly affect other areas of our lives.

The preceding nine sections define the new monetary, financial, and economic paradigm as a mega-paradigm change.

Only two mega paradigm changes have occurred in human history. The first was the emergence of human self-awareness, and the second was from Nomadic Hunting and

Gathering to Agriculture, Homesteading and Urbanization. The new monetary, financial, and economic paradigm of Abundantly Direct and Reciprocal Monetary Gifting will be the third such mega paradigm change.

That is an incredibly relevant, powerful, and joyous personal fact that should motivate us all to become involved in implementing it.

The Key Insights to Take from This Book

1. The most important thing about the policies of Wisdomics-Gracenomics is

actually not just their wonderful monetary and economic effects...it's how those policies will be able to help everyone self-actualize the many beneficial aspects of the natural philosophical concept and experience of grace, and also how those policies will enable businesses to turn from mere self-interest and happily join in the effort of creating the many greater survival aspects of the natural philosophical concept of grace in the interests of ecological sanity,

planetary survival and higher consciousness itself, which in the end is the best, highest and most direct benefit of the experience of grace. Wisdomics-Gracenomics' greatest effect will be its universally participated in consciousness raising effects of making the infrastructure of the economy an opportunity to self-actualize the experience of grace as in gratitude.
2. Paradigm changes are much more progressive and significant events than mere

theories which are less integrative levels of thought.
3. A paradigm is a single concept that creates an entirely new pattern.
4. Everything in the body of knowledge/area of human endeavor that a new paradigm applies to adapts to the new paradigm, and not the other way around.
5. Paradigmatic thinking is the highest order of integrative thinking. It takes the particles of truth in opposing theories in the body of knowledge a new paradigm applies to, and along with a

new deep insight creates a genuine thirdness greater oneness of those truths. It is essentially the same state of mind as wisdom thinking because the process of gaining and garnering wisdom is the integration of only the truths, highest workability's, best applicability's and the highest ethical considerations of opposing perspectives.

6. It can be verified that aspects of the natural philosophical concept of grace have always been the

primary effects in all historical paradigm changes.

7. The natural philosophical concept of grace is the pinnacle concept of wisdom, and wisdom is always imminently applicable. Otherwise, it wouldn't be wisdom. Monetary grace as in gifting embodied in the philosophy and policies of Wisdomics-Gracenomics is hence a reflective aspect of grace applied to the economy; and the concept of the new monetary and financial paradigm aligns with the historical trend that

aspects of grace define new paradigms.

8. The 50% Discount/Rebate policy at the point of retail sale is the very expression of the new paradigm and would affect the new paradigm all by itself. In conjunction with its paired policy of a universal dividend and the rest of the policies and regulations of Wisdomics-Gracenomics the economic and monetary effects of the paradigm change would be synergized and made stably permanent.

	Tying the 50% discount/rebate policy to the point of retail sale simultaneously resolves the two deepest and most chronic problems of modern economies, namely a scarcity of both individual incomes and systemic business revenue, and chronic inflation. This means that we can pour virtually as much money directly into the hands of the individual and toward the research and development of necessary programs to confront converging crises as

we so desire because the 50% discount/rebate policy integrates price deflation beneficially into profit making economic systems. And remember, hyperinflations never occur except under prior extreme circumstances...none of which presently exist and all of which can be artfully avoided.
9. Understanding the effects of the 50% discount/rebate policy is a paradigm changing realization in and of itself.

10. Retail sale is presently the only legitimate ending point of the economic/productive process. Thus, any additional cost post retail sale is economically illegitimate. Thus, money creation that only adds cost to the economy and individuals is not a legitimate business model at all, but rather a parasite on the actually productive economy. Unless we implement the Gifting/Debt Jubilee policy at the point of loan signing.
11. Current macro-economics being a new body of

knowledge, has a very short cultural horizon and so does not perceive the glaringly contradictory monopoly paradigm wielding power that private finance in an allegedly competitive free market system. Most macro-economists do not understand the money creation process into which private finance has parasitically and integrally entwined itself within the economic process. Neither does it perceive the illegitimacy of additional costs post retail sale. Hence

it does not recognize private banking/finance as a dominating business model.
12. Private finance, with elite banks that have a monopoly paradigm of Debt Only as the sole form and vehicle for the creation and distribution of money also flies in the face of the wisdom of Lord Acton's dictum that "Power corrupts, and absolute power corrupts absolutely."
13. The private financial system will always have the temptations and problems it currently has…unless it is aligned with and firmly

guided by the policies and regulations of Wisdomics-Gracenomics which are firmly guided by the natural philosophical concept and ethic of grace as in benevolent and yet sovereign power.

14. The banking and financial system should become a fourth branch of government with full separation of powers from the other three branches. The primary policies and regulations of a universal dividend, twin 50% discount/rebate policies at

retail sale and also at note signing should become new constitutional amendments.

15. The new monetary paradigm, intelligently implemented, is the only way we are going to "get off the dime" toward enabling all green consumer items to become easily purchased. It is also the way to be able to fund all the mega projects necessary to survive the end of petroleum and the climate change crisis as well.

16. Virtually all the signatures of imminent historical paradigm changes are

present now, and Wisdomics-Gracenomics fulfills all the accomplished signatures of historical paradigm changes.

17. All the policy suggestions of the leading heterodox economists and theorists philosophically align with Wisdomics-Gracenomics yet none of them approach let alone complete a paradigm change as does Wisdomics-Gracenomics.

18. It's all about a new paradigm. A new theory is a couple levels of understanding and

effectiveness below a new paradigm. Economic theories are mere reforms instead of a complete pattern change. A new theory that ignores the monetary and financial paradigm doesn't go deep enough and so the dominant powers always game it, work around it and undo its reforms as we've seen with Keynesianism morphed into the present dominant theory of neo-classical macro-economics.

19. Everything within the body of knowledge/area of human

endeavor adapts to the new paradigm and not the other way around. A paradigm is a pattern, and a new paradigm creates a new pattern of such significance that it becomes primary.

20. We are many and the political and money system elites are few.
21. The new monetary and financial paradigm will be only the third mega-paradigm change in human history. A mega-paradigm change is one that immediately, continually, and personally affects the

individual, and also has "knock on" beneficial effects in areas not directly related to the specific area of the new paradigm. The only other mega-paradigm changes were when humans became self-aware and the change from Hunting and Gathering to Agriculture, Homesteading and Urbanization.

The Mass Movement Necessary for the Political Implementation of Wisdomics-Gracenomics and How You Can Help Make It Possible

It has been attributed to Victor Hugo for having written: "There is one thing stronger than all the armies in the world, and that is an idea whose time has come."

And that is why the paradigm changing ideas and policies of Wisdomics-Gracenomics must become a mass movement that awakens the general populace, and together we will get them politically implemented.

The real problem we face isn't the lack of benefits or ability to resolve long standing problems of the new monetary and financial paradigm as described in this book. Rather it is the lack of vision to see it and then build a movement to make it our reality.

Every new paradigm conceived in human existence has ultimately been a political fight. I'm sure the witch doctors and tribal leaders of Hunting and Gathering societies told the people who decided to stop roaming that they were going to die because "everybody knows" you have to go find game, find the sporadic groves with low hanging fruit and grab it until it's gone and then you move on. But when they came back next year after being predated, more often than not suffering from malnutrition, suffering from the effects of exposure, and they saw virtually everybody who stayed in one place happy, warm and prosperous...the leaders lost some more of the community until over the centuries the new paradigm came fully into being.

Martin Luther King, Jr. and Mohandas Gandhi recognized the necessity of peaceful mass movements to move the political apparatus toward sanity and ethics. Let us follow their examples.

Today we have social media, and we have a system that is unstable and about to become precariously so if we do not swiftly act to benefit everyone with these policies and regulations. Students are saddled with major debt, asset inflation forces everyone to incur higher and higher levels of debt if they want a home, and both the individual and the vast majority of enterprise are afflicted by both the scarcity of individual income and so business revenue, and last but not least they are forced into the straight jacket of continual growth instead of abundant degrowth. Meanwhile the disruptive force of artificial intelligence is poised to eliminate a high percentage of current jobs.

It is time for advance. It is time for permanent progress. It is time for the new paradigm of Abundantly Direct and Reciprocal Monetary Gifting that will enable everyone to have a more broadly purposeful lifestyle and the monetary resources and the leisure time to enjoy it.... for their entire adult life. It is also time to proceed with post haste toward ecological sanity which the new paradigm also enables.

Let us join together to demand and command the political elites to end the oppressive 5000-year-old paradigm of Debt Only and implement the new paradigm so that we may have greater life, liberty, rationality and the pursuit of happiness via wealth and deeper purpose.

Please alert all your social media friends to this book and its policies, and also go to my patreon page and contribute at least $1/mo. so that we can build the mass movement to get these policies enacted. Thank you.

https://www.patreon.com/user?u=4749561

https://stevehummel.substack.com/publish

These insights enlighten the elemental fact that paradigm changes are deep simplicities, that is, they are single concepts that change entire patterns, and that simplicity, not complexity, is the key to perceiving paradigms and their consciousness raising effect.

www.ingramcontent.com/pod-product-compliance
Lightning Source LLC
Chambersburg PA
CBHW072030230526
45466CB00020B/1206